# The Wedekind Cabaret

by

Eric Bentley

FOUNDED 1830

NEW YORK HOLLYWOOD LONDON TORONTO

SAMUELFRENCH.COM

Cover illustrations: a drawing of Wedekind by Orlik confronts
a drawing of Eric Bentley by Lamont O'Neal

Copyright © 2008 by Eric Bentley

ALL RIGHTS RESERVED

CAUTION: Professionals and amateurs are hereby warned that *THE WEDEKIND CABARET* is subject to a royalty. It is fully protected under the copyright laws of the United States of America, the British Commonwealth, including Canada, and all other countries of the Copyright Union. All rights, including professional, amateur, motion picture, recitation, lecturing, public reading, radio broadcasting, television and the rights of translation into foreign languages are strictly reserved. In its present form the play is dedicated to the reading public only.

The amateur live stage performance rights to *THE WEDEKIND CABARET* are controlled exclusively by Samuel French, Inc., and royalty arrangements and licenses must be secured well in advance of presentation. PLEASE NOTE that amateur royalty fees are set upon application in accordance with your producing circumstances. When applying for a royalty quotation and license please give us the number of performances intended, dates of production, your seating capacity and admission fee. Royalties are payable one week before the opening performance of the play to Samuel French, Inc., at 45 W. 25th Street, New York, NY 10010.

Royalty of the required amount must be paid whether the play is presented for charity or gain and whether or not admission is charged.

Stock royalty quoted upon application to Samuel French, Inc.

For all other rights than those stipulated above, apply to: Broadway Bound Productions, 300 West 55th Street, Ste.1500, New York, NY 10019 Att: Jeff Britton.

Particular emphasis is laid on the question of amateur or professional readings, permission and terms for which must be secured in writing from Samuel French, Inc.

Copying from this book in whole or in part is strictly forbidden by law, and the right of performance is not transferable.

Whenever the play is produced the following notice must appear on all programs, printing and advertising for the play: "Produced by special arrangement with Samuel French, Inc."

Due authorship credit must be given on all programs, printing and advertising for the play.

ISBN 978-0-573-66025-2   Printed in U.S.A.   #25642

No one shall commit or authorize any act or omission by which the copyright of, or the right to copyright, this play may be impaired.

No one shall make any changes in this play for the purpose of production.

Publication of this play does not imply availability for performance. Both amateurs and professionals considering a production are strongly advised in their own interests to apply to Samuel French, Inc., for written permission before starting rehearsals, advertising, or booking a theatre.

No part of this book may be reproduced, stored in a retrieval system, or transmitted in any form, by any means, now known or yet to be invented, including mechanical, electronic, photocopying, recording, videotaping, or otherwise, without the prior written permission of the publisher.

**IMPORTANT BILLING AND CREDIT REQUIREMENTS**

All producers of *THE WEDEKIND CABARET must* give credit to the Author of the Play in all programs distributed in connection with performances of the Play, and in all instances in which the title of the Play appears for the purposes of advertising, publicizing or otherwise exploiting the Play and/or a production. The name of the Author *must* appear on a separate line on which no other name appears, immediately following the title and *must* appear in size of type not less than fifty percent of the size of the title type.

*The Wedekind Cabaret* is dedicated to the memory
of my friend and collaborator Arnold Black (1923-2000)

# NOTES

My English versions of Wedekind's two great plays, *Spring's Awakening* and *The First Lulu* are in print with Applause Theatre Books. In the notes to the latter, the following item appears:

> 1993: Eric Bentley writes *The Wedekind Cabaret*, an entertainment made up of approximations in English of Wedekind' poems and songs.

Under the title *Tingle Tangle*, it was staged a year later by Isaiah Sheffer at The Ballroom, a club on west 28th street in Manhattan, with two actors, Alvin Epstein and Elise Stone. Excerpts were published in magazines on both sides of the Atlantic.

Fourteen years later, I am re-arranging the material used in *Tingle Tangle* and adding to it, the result being the two cabaret programs printed here. They are but a suggested re-arrangement, which may fill the amount of time available to a given producer, and which may suit his performers. Producers are free to produce either program without the other, or even, at need, to move items from one program to the other. There are of course simple structural ideas here which should not be abandoned: It is essential that "Program One" begin with the "Spring's Awakening Ballad" and end with the "Lulu Ballad." "Program Two" consists, essentially, of two longish stories: songs precede and follow them and also divide them one from the other.

I have mentioned that our cast at The Ballroom consisted of two actors, a man and a woman. Either program is best cast that way, but could also be a one man show – for a male actor, perhaps made up as Frank Wedekind and purporting to exhibit him in action in a Munich cabaret around 1900. About dividing up the songs: if an artist of each sex is available, it will be noted that some of the poems are obviously spoken or sung by a man, others by a woman, though yet others can plausibly be handled by either sex. As for the stories: "The Inoculation" is a monologue for a male, "The Sacrificial Lamb" could be half-dramatized so that we hear the voices of two actors, one male, one female.

Music? All of the prose in the show and some of the verse is to be spoken, not sung. A balance between spoken and sung material should be the aim. A piano-vocal score for *The Wedekind Cabaret*, available to producers from Samuel French, includes songs by four composers: Arnold Black, William Bolcom, Peter Winkler, and Lucas Mason.

About two poems (songs) in Program Two: "Love's Old Sweet Song" and "To Tilly:" Wedekind wrote the first when he was nineteen: the object of his love was not a girl but one of his aunts. The second was written as he lay dying in 1918. Tilly was his wife. There is a tenderness in Program Two largely absent from Program One.

–*Eric Bentley*

# CONTENTS

### Program One:

(Maximum content is here listed. Items unsuitable to a given performer can be dropped. The order of the songs [or spoken poems] is also flexible)

Moritat I: Spring's Awakening
Cabaret
Modern Girl
Astarte
Lulu
The Love Market
Ilse
My Cathy
My Lisa
Cora
Earth Spirit
Rosie
To a Hypochondriac
The Other
On my Bed of Ease
To a Cruel Beloved
Venus Duplex
Beautiful Boy
Ganymede
All Conquering Love
Realistic Rosetta
Mother
The Aunt Murderer
Franziska F.
The Teacher from Old Vienna
Nietzsche
Falling Apart
Comfort-in-Wartime
The Blind Boy
Comfort at all Times
Old Song
The Seven Sayings
To Myself
Pagliacci
Moritat II: Lulu

## Program Two

Dancing the Tingle Tangle
The Inoculation
Courtship
Conquest
Love's Old Sweet Song
To Tilly
The Sacrificial Lamb
Eros Two

(Program Two is shorter only on the Contents page. The Inoculation is a long monologue. Equally long, The Sacrificial Lamb can either be another monologue or a piece for two readers.)

# THE WEDEKIND CABARET

## PROGRAM ONE

Two original ballads and 32 Wedekind poems and songs

## MORITAT I
## SPRING'S AWAKENING

Here's a mini-Reign-of-Terror
War uncivil to the knife
Which beset three little people
In the springtime of their life.

See these children in the schoolyard
Of an ancient German town!
Watch their games and hear their voices!
And observe what shot them down.

Hark to Melchior and Moritz
And to Wendla, Melchi's friend.
Two of them knew springtime's pleasures.
Two met with a frightful end.

Melchi's fourteen, Wendla's thirteen.
Winter now his exit makes.
They're together in a hayloft.
Thunderclap! The spring awakes!

When she said No, did she mean it?
Melchi did not say she lied
And when, later, people asked him:
Was it rape? Yes, he replied.

And the tryst had consequences.
Wendla did not feel quite well.
Ma, who recognized the symptoms,
Thought her daughter bound for hell:

How keep her from Satan's clutches?
Save her from the infernal pit?
Ma admitted she was flummoxed
Then remembered: Mother Schmidt.

Smitty is the local midwife:
In your home or in her room
She can bring to birth a baby
Or destroy it in the womb.

And when people tell Old Smitty
Baby is a child of sin
She provides the Smitty Tablets
That will do the infant in.

And sometimes the Smitty Tablets
Do more than they're asked to do.
Killing little Wendla's offspring
They took care of Wendla too.

On a charge of rape and rapine
Melchior now went to jail
While his classmate Moritz Stiefel –
Hear it, folks, and weep! Turn pale!

For the timid, wide-eyed Moritz
Spring's awakening was grim
No threat to the girls like Melchi,
Girls, he felt, were threatening him

For while Melchi had fared onward
In his spring's awakening
Moritz had fared ever inward
Into dire imagining:

Life's too much! He cannot take it!
What he does take is a gun.
Sticks the barrel 'twixt his teeth and
Blows his head up at the sun.

Where stands Melchi now?
0 horror! Both his friends have died on him.
"Sink or swim?" Young Melchi queries
And prepares to sink, not swim.

And now something spooky happened:
Melchior to the graveyard came
First thing that he saw – you guessed it –
 On a headstone: WENDLA'S NAME –

Near the stone, the ghost of Moritz,
Underneath his arm, his head.
And near Moritz a MASKED STRANGER
Screams as if to wake the dead:

MELCHI, DO NOT FOLLOW MORITZ!
COME BACK FROM THAT DREADFUL BRINK!
Sink or swim! Dive in and swim, lad,
Swim so that you CANNOT sink!

Moritz and the STRANGER vanish.
Wendla's corpse will ne'er grow warm.
Melchi meets the STRANGER'S challenge
And strides out into the storm.

MORAL
When your daughter is eleven
 – On her body signs of spring –
Let her (if she'd get to heaven)
Study SPRING'S AWAKENING.

## OTHER NEWS

Not all whom the spring awakened
Killed themselves or broke the law.
Hansi bought some picture postcards,
Lovely ladies in the raw:

And he dreamed he was Othello
Murd'ring Desdemona sweet
As he flushed the naked ladies
Down below his toilet seat –

Thus did Hans remove temptation,
But, returning now to class,
Noticed that his classmate Ernest
Had a photogenic ass.

"May I take your picture, Ernest?
In the nude would be just fine!"
Rolling in the grass together
They invented sixty'nine.

## CABARET
### (from Tingel-Tangel)

Yes, it's true, love is my credo
Eros has me in his grip
And (oh dear) I'm a torpedo
For many a pocket battleship.

Look me in the face and tell me
What it is you read therein:
Is it not, my friend, that virtue
Really is a deadly sin?

So: an end to all the bleating!
The Ideal has blown away!
(But the heart of man's still beating
In the Schwabing cabaret.)

**MODERN GIRL**
**(2 stanzas from)**

A different drum has set the pace
She does not fake it
In step with new times
She dances naked.

The devil has done his damnedest
To keep her indoors, a lady of leisure
World and woman go out in the storm
Such is God's pleasure.

For world and woman exchange a glance
Then hand in hand together advance
And dance!

**ASTARTE**

Astarte, this my prayer to thee:
Take my virginity from me!
My innocence is but a curse
That only goes from bad to worse.
Astarte, I'm alone each night
Take pity, goddess, on my plight.

I bite the pillow
Shred my nightgown
The moon and thou
Look coldly down.

Astarte, I'm fifteen already
Hair is growing on my body.
Unfamiliar feelings ripple
Through the breast and to the nipple
I've offered thee, through this past year,
Sacrifice of my blood so dear.

The monthly plan
Of the moon and thee
Is afoot – inside me.
My body cries out for a man.

## LULU

Some people love a dog's life
It has regularity.
I love the heaving seesaw
Of this world's raging sea.

Enduring science, living art,
Love is what I love:
Firstfruits of the earth below
Manna from heaven above.

If a man gives me the feeling
I'm strong, I'm splendid, I'm a success
I'll jump for joy and, shouting,
Uncover my nakedness.


## THE LOVE MARKET
**(from Confession )**

God may lash me for it but I swore
And swear again now in his Holy Name
I would much prefer to be a whore
To having all their happiness and fame.

World, you lost in me a worldly woman
I had no objection at all to sin.
Who so at home in the Love Market
As I would have been?

There are some who live for their profession
Me I live for love. But why
Should I love just once and then get stuck with
This one particular guy?

For loving does not bring us happiness
It brings jealousy and degradation.
But to *be* loved, strongly, hotly, often,
That is living! That is exaltation!

**ILSE**

A child of fourteen I had never
Had anything to do with boys
But that's when I made a discovery':
Sweet as sugar are love's joys.

He laughed and took hold of my body
This is not gonna hurt! he said
Then he gently, gently pushed my
Underskirt over my head.

Since then my life has all been springtime:
And I make love with one and all
And if the time comes no man wants me
I'm ready for my funeral.


**MY CATHY**

My Cathy requests – as a bonus –
A love poem from me.
O spare me, Cathy, I answer
For I simply cannot agree.

And do I really love you?
I am not sure that's it.
You say that is beside the point?
Well, Cathy, hold on a bit:

When I, my dear, write love poems
It's early in the night
Because, my dear, on the day after,
It is too hard to write.

## MY LISA

Has Lisa had on any panties
Since the end of March? No, she has not
But that is because, here in April,
It gets so infernally hot.

This circumstance got me to thinking
And here is what entered my mind:
To make her a gift of some panties
The gauzy diaphanous kind.

Adown the street hopping and skipping
She might catch cold, don't you agree?
A cold is no cosmic disaster
But one should behave prudently.


## CORA

Behold the breakwater, it stretches
Between the breakers blue
And I myself stretch out between
Your bridegroom and you.

How pleasant to doze off upon
Such neutral territory!
It's life in Switzerland midway between
Prussia and Sicily.

Icy shivers run down my back
 – Hail, snow, etcetera –
What's stretching out before me
Glowing and hot? Italia.

## EARTH SPIRIT

The wages of sin is enjoyment:
Go to it! Sin! Be wild!
Or do you need assistance?
Are you still a child?

Earth's treasures are *there*, why shun them?
Seize them with pride.
Spurn the laws that bid you
Kick 'em aside.

Happy on fresh graves if you
Romp till you're out of breath!
Dance on the ladder to the gallows!
Why bore yourself to death?

## ROSIE

Rose was a mass of flesh, for sure,
But it was virtuous and pure.

He had a good head, Freddie Frick,
He had good hair too on his – .

When Rose took a walk in the woods nearby
Fred was already there. Oh my!

Said Freddie to himself, What luck
Here is a lass for me to

This lad, thought she, is after my –
Which is a thing I do not wunt.

She ran; he followed; what is more
His – was bigger than before.

Nimbly young Rosie made a rush
Toward the undergrowth 'neath an elder bush

For she had something to do therein
That ofttimes makes a resounding din.

As for Freddie, he was sure
She was only taking a water cure.

Opportunity makes the thief! said he
And crept towards her amorously.

When with a smirk he pinched her thigh
Fat Rosie finally let fly.

A din resounded. Fred was deflated
And the life force abdicated.

There's a moral in this? You're right:
A glow worm can't provide sunlight.

## TO A HYPOCHONDRIAC

You furrow your forehead
You curse and you swear
You swallow the worm
Along with the pear.

So sensitive are you
To what's mean and crude.
Be a child! And bid welcome
Nature's plenitude.

Your sweetheart is sour?
The sweeter her kiss –
The smaller her bedroom
The larger your bliss.

## THE OTHER

Love's pleasure and love's pain
Are nowhere forgotten so fast
As in the arms of another.

Your eyes were black, my dear,
Black was the cloud-capped night.
Blue were the eyes of the other.

Oh, no one could kiss as you could
Soft as a morning in May.
Hard was the kiss of the other.

You were unfaithful and false
But I can match that too:
I'm being betrayed by the other.

**ON MY BED OF EASE**

On my bed of ease reclining
I ask what my life has meant.
Did I miss the silver lining?
Why the discontent?

Don't I exist and get around.
Eat lunch, smoke cigarettes?
Don't the girls I like abound
Trollops and suffragettes?

Psychopathia sexualis?
For me, a youthful fad!
(Though what I can tell you all is
Some very good times were had.)

## TO A CRUEL BELOVED

Over the hills, O huntress fleet,
Run your beagle pack!
When they come back
Smothered, I bet,
With dust and sweat
Get out your whip
And let 'er rip!
They'll whimper and lick your feet.

So, Artemis, tell
Who shall ever break your spell?
Will your leash ever give way?
When you blow your horn, will your dogs ever, ever
    disobey?
Will you hear the soul's desperate cries?
Not before one dies,
Tendons, veins, and heart
Torn apart.

So swing your whip
And let 'er rip!
When, huntress, you
Shout: View, Halloo,
Death sings: my victory's forever
The eye, shot with blood and flame,
Looks out for the big game
Of your pleasure
(Big game indeed beyond measure)
But finds it – never.

## VENUS DUPLEX

1. What the Boy Sang

Seen from in front, you are the loveliest girl
That ever rescued me from love's despair
But when you turn your head, what do I see?
It seems to me you have become a boy.
So I stay close as if to Fortune's Wheel
To Venus Duplex, Venus Duplex – you.

2. What the Girl Sang

Seen from in front, you are a boy most fair
Who rescued me from love's despair
But when you turn your head, what do I see?
You are a girl, or so it seems to me.
You turn, my dear, you turn like Fortune's Wheel.
I will stand by you both for now I feel
That you are duplex – Venus Duplex – real.

## BEAUTIFUL BOY

All mankind may rant and rave
And throw me alive headfirst into my grave
But a slender boy
Brings me all the joy
I conspicuously fail
To get from a fat female.
And I have to confess my sin!
I just cannot hold it in
Though every old dame
From a house of ill fame
Go on the warpath
(Whore path).

It's almost a duty
To praise woman's beauty
And that of horses, dogs, flowers and greenery
The weather, landscape, seascape, almost any scenery
It's fine
To praise beauty even in swine:
Pigmarket in Haarlem is the name
Of a picture that brought Max Liebermann money and
    fame
But a boy – a slim
Boy, praise the beauty in him?
You're crossing yourself! You're thinking you ought
To scream: perish the thought!
And all mankind is of much the same mind.
(I never did think much of all mankind)

## GANYMEDE

So stretch out your legs, my comrade pretty!
Those stockings of black thread – from which Scotch city?–
Reach right up your thigh
When I pull them that high.

That's what's insidious about you,
The black stockings! Can I live without you?
Your skin shimmers through the wide mesh:
One longs to nibble at your flesh.

Those patent leather shoes of yours! And how
You lay one foot upon the other. Wow!
What bliss it would be to tie your laces –
I'm transported to heaven and such places.

Hair black and curly, cheeks pure white,
Mouth stark naked, black eyes full of fright
And deep! How splendid!
It's a wonder my life is not upended.

It's in your legs your great attraction lies.
I see you walk and tears come to my eyes.
Did I say walk? You sail, you float!
Your lissom ankles have me by the throat.

As a souvenir, for starters,
I'll give you delicate lilac garters.
(The coat of arms thereon's old hat
But then you're a lady – not just an aristocrat.)

A small boy's charms aren't lessened by a dime
If he dresses as a girl from time to time.
Know what your mother said to me?
You're "the incarnate spirit of chivalry"!

How well you do in your examinations!
Glamorous women give you palpitations –
I just love *that*! Let no man say
I undervalue you, cher protégé.

A cherub now, in a month or two
The bud will burst. Then you
Will look at me in horror and distress –
I'd stroked your hair with such tenderness!

A pity beauty doesn't last!
Even yours, your highness. Fast
Puberty makes you just another John.
Banal. The fragrance gone.

## ALL CONQUERING LOVE

Our culture just adores you, Miss.
You are sublime. We all agree.
You breed the bedbug, louse, and flea
Crabs, gonorrhea, syphilis.

The writing's on the wall? Ah no,
On *thee* our MENE TEKEL's writ.
Where falls thy shadow I am hit
And NAUSEA hath laid me low.

But when you float down from above
At nightfall, we ourselves deprave
And I become the loyal slave
Of your horrendous empire, Love.


## REALISTIC ROSETTA

Rosetta wants it understood:
Love is a pig, love is the pits.
And people do it, she admits,
Only because it feels so good.

And this the burden of her song:
All Conquering Love can surely kill,
One lover make the other ill.
(What they take in, they pass along.)

So: when some piglet would make love
To her, she wants it clearly seen
That, outside and in, the guy is clean
As angels in the sky above.

**MOTHER**

Who shot the sperm to the ovary
That brought to birth a wretch like me?
Upon my forehead I can read
It was not I that did the deed.

My lady mother was a slut,
Christ, what a – Fire and brimstone!! But
Samsons of every race and kind
When they quit her place left hair behind.

On the very morning that she bore
This son, my mother played the whore:
She was tossing ecstatic'ly with a man
Well after the labor pains began

And was still hotly clutching him
When on the bed fell the shadow grim
"I'm sorry to disturb but please,"
Said the Grim Reaper, "stop it! Cease!"

Moral

So everyone asks, who was it hurled
Myself into an astonished world?
Heaven, give him misery on this earth
And have him give me a wide, wide berth!

## THE AUNT MURDERER

Auntie was old and feeble
And I butchered her where she lay
Rummaged in her chest of drawers
Being there for an overnight stay.

In the chest I found golden treasure
And all her securities too
While Auntie snored and gasped for air –
A tactless unfeeling thing to do!

What good all her fretting and fuming?
Around me was blackest night.
When I stabbed her in the gut with the dagger
Auntie gave up the fight.

The cash weighed a lot. So did Auntie.
I grabbed her by her nightgown.
I had noted a vent to the cellar.
My hand shook as I pushed her down.

Auntie was old and feeble
I butchered her and ran.
You judges are now after MY life?
But I'm such a young young man!

*In the German, the second stanza is ambiguous. It could
be the speaker who is tactless and unfeeling. In which case an
English version could read:*

I found there a pile of securities
Also a heap of gold
And when Auntie snored and gasped for air
I was unfeeling and cold.

## FRANZISKA F.

There was a young girl called Franziska:
When she to Baden-Baden came
She found a job in a boutique and
Won for herself an honest name.

Her boss, a lady somewhat older.
Devoted to that shop was she.
Her husband was a functionary
Of the Royal Railway Companee.

One night the lady said at supper:
Franziska, go to this address
And carry, please, this parcel with you
And give it to the Baroness.

But on the way Franziska met with
An Individual who said:
Unless you do me one small favor
I'll put a bullet through my head.

She, inexperienced, and not wishing
To see him perish at her feet
Said Yes. He later stole her parcel
And left her standing in the street.

At first she could not comprehend it
Then she began to sob and cry:
I was seduced! she told her mistress.
Her mistress said, That is no lie.

But since a bustle had been stolen
The bustle of a Baroness
Her heart got hardened to Franziska:
By now she could not like her less.

Franziska pleaded for forgiveness:
For, unforgiven, what would betide her?
That night she slept, though, with that In-
-dividual in bed beside her.

At Whitsun when her lord and lady
Had with the Singers' Club left town
Without a moment's hesitation
She said to him: so come on down.

She showed him round. He took a fancy
To desk, cash-register and such
And helped himself to sundry papers
Not bothering to thank her much.

And when Franziska realized what
Her boyfriend had just done that day
She bade farewell to lord and lady
And on tiptoe she crept away.

Two days ago she was in prison
We are not free to tell you where.
The young man who had started all this
By yesterday was also there.

## THE TEACHER FROM OLD VIENNA

In Vienna lived a teacher
Siggie Sousa was his name
Just as fine a guy as ever
To those precincts ever came.

Was a husband and a father
Had three children still quite small
But alas he was not happy
Didn't like his life at all.

That his wife was ever faithful
Sigismund could never see
He suspected that another
Fathered all the children three.

Jealousy tormented Siggie
And deluded this good man
Till convinced that he'd been cheated,
He devised a Master Plan.

Write me a confession! Quoth he
Late one night unto his wife
Then dictated the confession
That would cost his wife her life.

As the woman named the father
Of her kiddies (now in bed)
He took aim at all three of 'em
Took good aim and shot them dead.

Whereupon he forced the lady
Down on that same bed to lie
Though she begged him and implored him
She too must lie down and die.

And when frightfully our friend
Shot himself, that was the end.

A neighbor, hearing the shots in the night,
Kicked in the door and turned on the light.
You can imagine the horror of his report
To the Court.

> *(To be sung to the tune of She Was Poor But She Was Honest, except for the last six lines which are spoken.)*

**NIETZSCHE**

What good can these sleepy limbs do me?
What help from this drunken brain?
As soon as the lamp has sputtered out
The bedbugs are back again.

Hypochondria drowns in wine
Like Pharaoh's horde in the sea
But from these hordes of bedbugs
What red flood shall rescue me?

I douse the lamp beside my cot.
I'm groaning, I'm so itchy,
It's in this mood, my pride forgot,
That I flee with a curse to Nietzsche.

**FALLING APART**

After one last look at my old hymn book
I tossed it into the sea.
Goodbye, goodbye, angels on high!
Welcome, debauchery!

I called my God a sleepy old sod
And, laughing when these words shocked Him,
I called the old beaver UNHOLY DECEIVER
Then out of His temple I locked Him.

His gleaming shrine was now all mine!
Was I mad or glad? It was odd –
A blissful abyss – an abysmal bliss –
Had made me a beast and a god!

I stay overnight at the altar bright
Full of murderous thoughts to the brim
Supine on the altar, I whimsic'ly slaughter
Myself– a burnt offering to Him.

## THE BLIND BOY

O my childhood, days of childhood
That have vanished into night
When the Soul still lived in blindness
And the Eye was full of light–
And its gaze, I let it wander –
On each face I let it fall
Took belief for understanding
And had no thoughts, none at all.

Till one day, what was I doing?
Was I falling down a well?
Did a tidal wave within me
Angrily begin to swell?
I was thinking! Gazing inward!
Flowing toward my Soul in streams!
Nevermore would I gaze outward
Toward the bright sun's golden beams!

Now I must despise a world which
Late had seemed God's garden fair:
He leaves the good to languish in it.
The bad all sing his praises there.
Gone now is the joy of childhood!
Gone the fun! The peace of mind!
My Soul had learned to do the seeing
And behold! my Eyes went blind.

**COMFORT AT ALL TIMES**

Death comes soon and is certain
He's waiting down the years
A Comforter, though scary,
In this vale of tears.

From love I do not hate him
I love him hotly from hate
Because to live forever
Would be a gruesome fate.

Eternal Return: feed the body
Then funnel the fodder through it
The ultimate product: faeces
My ultimate wish: to quit.

**OLD SONG**

Oh, there was once a baker
His great big paunch was his pride
One saw him strutting and showing
It off on every side.

He took to wife a woman
She too was built like that
They could not come together
For they were much too fat.

## THE SEVEN SAYINGS

I
I who am I: the All Powerful
I am the Hidden One who created thee for his pleasure
My joys are thy sufferings
My life is thy death.

II
Thou shalt not call the earth thine own
Nor fire nor water nor horse nor hound
Nor father nor mother nor wife nor child.

III
Go hunting for thy food if need be
But despise not work.
Better to hunt and catch nothing than to find
Thou art thyself the hunted:
Feed, rather, on thy work.

IV
Mortify not the flesh for the soul's sake
Rather, for thy body's sake mortify thy soul!
For the soul has to fear the soul's suffering
While the body's sufferings are most splendid sacrifices.

V
I who am I created the human being to die
I who am I gave thee lust that thou needest not fear death
Thou who satest thy lust on death.
Woe to him who sateth his lust on worser food:
He will rot in darkness.

VI
Hold sacred the games of children
And disturb them not!
In them is neither idleness nor folly.

## VII
Thou shalt not make love out of lust
But out of strength and self-confidence!
Thou shalt not make love in the dark but in the light!
Woe to the love that dies when human beings see it!
As thy love is shall thy children be.
To love in the dark is to live in the dark.

## TO MYSELF

So you're suffering physical harm?
Act! Don't stand there and talk!
If you've been happy recently
Take up thy bed and walk!

Thine eye offends thee? Pluck it out
Lest both thine eyes offend!
Your problem's a nagging wife in the house?
The solution's divorce, my friend.

Yes, prayer and fasting are stupid.
Align the wood. Plane it. Make do.
Don't let Weltschmerz poetry
Be all that's expected of you.

## PAGLIACCI
*(from King Nicolo)*

Strange how moody and capricious
This our life! One wonders why.
I am mostly so astonished
I can neither laugh nor cry.

If the universe around us
Has no center as they say
Then the best a man can do is:
Turn one somersault a day.

If your agile legs are aided
By your arms' agility
You'll embrace even misfortune
And make friends with misery.

## MORITAT II
## LULU

She was born in the big city
In the middle of a slum
Chap called Shig passed for her papa
And a harlot was her mum.

And when she was six or seven
Gent called Shunning and no fool
Washed her, dressed her, combed her, groomed her
Placed her in a classy school.

At sixteen or maybe sooner
She was Shunning's joy and pride.
Did we tell you he was married?
He had Lulu on the side.

Set her up too with a husband
Doc of Med'cine name of Goll
When the doc was at the clinic
She was Frankie Shunning's moll.

Doctor Goll he hired a painter
Name of Quartz or Schwartz or so
He would capture Lulu's beauty
On his canvas, make it glow.

Oh these painters with their models!
Always get them into bed.
That's what Schwartsy did with Lulu.
When he found out, Goll dropped dead.

Lulu got his dough, and Schwartsy
He got Lulu for a wife.
He was oh so very happy
Till he heard about her life.

Shunning's first wife died and Shunning
Had a second wife in view
Wished to be so faithful to her
That he'd have to drop Lulu.

After all, she had a husband,
What need Shunning on the side?
But when Schwartsy got the message
He committed suicide.

What an awkward situation!
Shun can't marry like he said.
No, he's gonna buckle down and
Marry our Lulu instead.

Shunning had a son called Alva
(After Thomas Edison).
On the wedding day our Lulu
Went to bed with Shunning's son.

Shun became a morphine addict
And then with his ev'ry breath
He resolved to end the story
With the lovely Lulu's death.

Lulu's death! Should Shunning kill her?
If he did so, he'd be through.
He must chat with her, persuade her
She herself the deed must do.

Or must she? The lovely Lulu
Gamely gave Shun's plan a try.
Made her want to go on living.
It was Shunning who must die!

She put one, two bullets in him –
Newspapers would call it three –
Then to 'scape police and prison
Ran away to Gay Paree.

In Montmartre lovely Lulu
Found a house of much ill fame.
Alva Shun was now her husband.
Countess D'Oubra was her name.

In Paree had many lovers
One, a famous Fancy Man
Posed as an Italian Marquis.
He too had a little plan:

Lulu now would move to Cairo
Scene of Oriental lore
And in a luxurious whorehouse
She would be a luxury whore.

"Fuck with ev'ry man that pays me?
No, no, no, that is not me!"
"I'll tell the cops you murdered Shunning
If you don't at once agree!"

Now the fat is in the fire!
What can lovely Lulu do?
This time she don't have no money
Only has, as helpers two

Alva and her father Shiggy
(If this rascal is her dad)
All three of them flee to London:
See what there can now be had.

Cold and broke, all three are starving
But says Shig (still full o'fun):
Let the now unlovely Lulu
Walk the streets of Albion!

'Twas the time of Jack the Ripper
Exact dates not known to us
But we know he butchered prosties
And cut out the uterus.

On the first and last occasion
Lu agreed to play the whore
Her first John said. let's get filthy!
Lu said: moi, je fais l'amour.

Second john was – dare we say it?
Second john– 0 world take note!
Second john – how shall we play it?
Second john – he cut her throat.

Was it Jack? There is no knowing.
Jack remains a mystery.
That her uterus was missing
Cops and medicos agree.

(And that night another girl was
Butchered by that butcher man.
It was she who most loved Lulu:
Countess Gesh, the Lesbian.)

MORAL
Lovely ladies, man adoring,
Learn from lovely Lulu's fate:
Don't decide to go out whoring
When the Ripper's at the gate.

# THE WEDEKIND CABARET

## PROGRAM TWO

Two original songs, two Wedekind stories and four Wedekind poems

## DANCING THE TINGLE TANGLE

And the bells go jingle jangle
In the Schwabing cabaret
As we dance the Tingle Tangle
At the closing of the day.

I see how men and women wrangle
And can neither laugh nor cry
Tingle always leads to tangle
I've tried all day to figure why.

Tangle always follows tingle
Quoth the poet with a sigh
Praps it's better to stay single
Virgin till the day you die?

As for us who have stayed single
None of us would dare deny
Tangle always follows tingle
We agree – gay, straight, or bi.

We had found nor why nor wherefore
By the closing of the day.
We dance the Tingle Tangle therefore
In the Schwabing cabaret.

## THE INOCULATION

If, my dear friends, I tell you this story, it is not because I want to provide a new example of woman's cunning or man's stupidity. I tell it, rather, because it contains certain psychological oddities which will interest you and everyone – from which indeed mankind, when aware of them, can derive considerable profit. Above all I would like, at the outset, to repudiate the idea that I am trying to make something of my own misdeeds back in those days ~ of that frivolity which today I regret from the depths of my soul, and for whose practice, now my hair is grey and my knees wobble, neither the desire nor the capability remains.

"My dear, sweet boy, you have nothing to be afraid of," Fanny said to me one fine evening when her husband had just come home, "for husbands, by and large, are jealous only as long as they have no reason to be. From the moment they are given an actual reason to be jealous, they are stricken with incurable blindness."

"I don't trust the expression on his face," I rejoined, feeling a little put down. "It seems to me he must have noticed something."

"You misunderstand, dear boy," said she. "His facial expression results from a procedure I adopted to stop him being jealous of you once and for all – to guarantee that he would never feel the least tremor of suspicion." "What kind of procedure?" I asked, astonished. "A kind of inoculation. On the very day when I decided to take you for my lover, I told him openly, to his face, that I love you. I then repeated it to him daily when he got up and when he went to bed. "You have every reason to be jealous of the dear boy," I tell him. "I love him from the bottom of my heart, and neither you nor I can take the credit if I haven't broken my marital vows. The fact that I have remained unshakably loyal is all his doing."

In this instant it was borne in on me why, often, her husband, in the midst of all manner of pleasantness with me, when he thought he was unobserved by me, would look at me with a smile that quite subtly combined compassion and contempt. "And do you really think this...procedure will work indefinitely?" I asked in some embarrassment. "It's infallible," she rejoined with all the self-assurance of an astronomer.

Nonetheless I entertained serious doubts as to the indubitability of her psychological calculations till one day the following event taught me better in an astonishing way.

At the time – in a narrow street of downtown Munich–I lived in a small furnished room on the fourth floor of a high apartment house, and it was my custom to sleep well into the day. One sunny morning at about nine the door opens, and she enters. What now follows I would never tell except that it offers the proof of one of the most surprising and yet credible delusions possible to the spiritual life of man.

She took everything off and pressed close to me. Don't expect me, dear friends, to be suggestive or risqué. I am not out–let me repeat–to regale you with improprieties. Scarcely had she pulled the sheet over her bodily charms than steps were heard at the door. A knock, and I have just time enough – with a quick movement – to pull the sheet over her head. Then her husband entered. Having climbed the 120 steps to my floor, he was out of breath and sweating heavily, yet his excited beaming face expressed nothing but joy.

"I wanted to ask if you'll go on a trip with Roebel, Schletter, and me. By train to Ebenhausen, then on bikes to Ammerland. Actually I wanted to work at home today but my wife went to the Bruechmanns to see how their youngest is doing, and the weather was so glorious I couldn't concentrate. I found Roebel and Schletter at Cafe Luitpold, and we made up a party. Our train leaves at 10.57."

I had meanwhile had time to collect my thoughts. "You can see," said I with a smile, "that I am not alone." "Yeah, I see that," he rejoined with the same understanding smile, whereupon his eyes started to twinkle and his jawbone shook up and down. Hesitantly he took a step forward and now stood right in front of the chair I used to keep my clothes on. On top lay a delicate sleeveless lace chemise – a name sewn into it in red – and over it two long black silk open-work stockings with golden clocks. Since nothing else of a feminine nature was to be seen, his eyes were fastened on these items of the female wardrobe with unmistakable lechery.

That was the decisive moment. One instant later and he would have to remember having seen these articles of clothing somewhere before. Cost what it may, I had to divert his attention from that fateful sight and somehow hold him transfixed so there would be no chance of his looking back. This goal, however, was only to be reached in a fashion entirely without precedent. The train of thought suddenly set going in my brain permitted me to perpetrate an act of such crudity that – though it saved the day – I have still not, after twenty years, forgiven myself for it.

"I am not alone," said I, "but if you had the least idea how splendid this creature is, you would envy me." Meanwhile my arm – the arm which had placed the sheet over her head – was rather hysterically pressed against the spot where I guessed her mouth was – in order, if you will, to take her breath away and prevent her giving any sign of life. Avidly his glances glided up and down along the wavy lines described by her sheet. And now it comes – the frightful, the unprecedented, occurrence. I took hold of the sheet at the bottom and pulled it up to her neck so that, now, only her head was covered. "Have you ever seen such magnificence in all your life?" I asked. His eyes opened wide yet he fell into visible embarrassment. "Yes, yes – well, I must say – you have very good taste – now, I – must be going – I'm so sorry I – disturbed you."

He was now moving back toward the door and, without any sign of haste, I pulled down the veil, then sprang quickly to my feet, and stuck myself in front of him by the door so it was impossible for him to see the stockings on the chair. "Anyway, I'm coming on the noon train to Ebenhausen," said I, as he held the latch in his hand. "Maybe you can wait for me at the Gasthof zur Post. We can then ride together to Ammerland. Marvellous trip, thanks so much for the invitation."

He then made a few well-meant, jovial-jocular remarks and left the room. I remained rooted to the spot till I heard his step down below in the lobby.

I will mercifully refrain from describing the state of fury and despair in which the deplorable woman found herself after this scene. Spiritually she went right off the rails, and provided me with such proofs of hatred and contempt as I had never received before. As she hastily got dressed, she threatened to spit in my face. I naturally abstained from any attempt to defend myself.

"So where are you thinking of going now?"

"Dunno – maybe I'll jump in the lake – or just go home – I could go to the Bruechmanns –see how their youngest is doing – Dunno."

By about two o'clock we were sitting together under the shady chestnut trees by the Gasthof zur Post in Ebenhausen, Roeben, Schletter, my friend and I, regaling ourselves on roast chicken and a juicy gleaming green salad. My friend, whose state of soul I was observing with some suspicion, set my mind at rest by his unusually cheerful mood He threw me jokingly significant looks and, chuckling, rubbed his hands together with a triumphant air, without however betraying what it was that was that affected him this way. The excursion went off without further disturbance, and toward ten in the evening we were back in town. Arriving at the station, we agreed to go to a beer garden.

"Just let me go home," said my friend, "and get my wife. She's been all day with that sick child and would take it amiss if we now leave her to spend the evening at home alone." Soon thereafter he arrived with her at the beer garden. The conversation naturally turned to the excursion whose actual uneventfulness was blown up by all of us into improbable tales of adventure.

The young woman was sparing of speech and a little helpless. She favored me with not a single look. He on the other hand exhibited in his jovial countenance that awareness of victory that had puzzled me before. His look of superiority and triumph was now directed less at me, however, than at the wife who was sitting there lost in her thoughts. It was as if he had experienced some inner, deeply satisfying blessing.

Not for a month afterwards – when I was alone with the young woman once again – was this riddle cleared up for me. I had first, of course, to hear once again all those wild complaints about my own behavior. Something of a reconciliation was then effected. This was difficult but she then confided in me that, when she came to be alone with her husband on the evening of that day, he made the following speech, folding his arms as he did so:

"My child, I have now got to know that dear, sweet boy of yours through and through. Every day that passes, you confess to me that you love him – without guessing what a laughing stock he is making of you. I saw him just this morning in his apartment. Naturally he was not alone. Yes, it was borne in upon me at that moment why he thinks so little of you and regards your feelings for him with contempt. The woman he loves has a body so bewitchingly, so overwhelmingly beautiful that you, with your relatively few charms, and those now somewhat faded, can hardly hope to offer any competition."

Such, my dear friends, was the effect of the inoculation. I'm telling you about it only so that in future you may be on guard against such magic potions.

## COURTSHIP

Let's play with the crazy fire of love
Down in the human depths where live
Jackals hyenas snakes whose teeth
Hound their wretched prey to death
Jungle beasts that then go mad
And gnaw at bodies already dead.
Tell the monstrous vermin this:
They can bite us as they wish!
Set barricades
At all the gates!
Let's lock
Ourselves in and fuck!


## CONQUEST

Oh dear, she won't let it happen!
Both her legs are saying No!
And though I've laid bare her bosom
She is covered up below.
And my eyes are gazing downward:
As they o'er those cov'rings play
I'm excited! But the lady
Shyly pushes me away.

Lady, I'm not going to force you!
Just give me a little kiss.
Your own wings will bear you, dear one,
From desire to final bliss.
Now, oh dear, she yields! And, smiling,
Says: Your kisses are a fright!
And, with both hands briskly fanning,
She puts out the candle light.

## LOVE'S OLD SWEET SONG

I love you, dear, does that get through to you?
The phrase is saccharine, so trite, so nice
Yet there is joy in it, there's happiness
I love you – there is paradise.

I love you, dearest, in the morning
The words call through the curtains with the light
And in the evening when the stars come out
I love you is what's singing in the night.

Should you be far away, I'm not complaining
You're in my heart and that is rather near
My soul rejoices and the words ring out
I LOVE YOU and I will not change, my dear...


## TO TILLY

A cruel and an angry fate
Rips apart us two.
Here, we only suffocate,
Nothing we can do.

Tilly, one last kiss for me!
What must be will be.

You are young. Warm blood wafts you
Toward happiness.
Fret not! Sojourn not with me
In the wilderness.

Tilly, one last kiss for me!
What must be will be.

I'm old and ailing. Comical.
A broken reed.
I never wished to while away the time
With an invalid.

Tilly, one last kiss for me!
What must be will be.

## THE SACRIFICIAL LAMB

*as a lamb to the slaughter....*
*as a sheep before her shearers...*
*cut off out of the land of the living...*

"No, please, don't ask me how I got here! How can you interest yourself in such a thing? Tomorrow you'll be laughing about it, I can see it in your face! Why try so hard to make me cry? It's much nicer for you if I'm cheerful!" And the slender Munich girl – very white, well-built, and with opulent, impenetrably thick black hair–bent trembling over him and kissed him on the mouth and on the halfclosed eyelashes trying to make him forget his question. It didn't work. He grimaced so that she shuddered from head to foot. He fought off her caresses and pushed her away, thus rendering her completely helpless, since her physical beauty was all she had in the world to call her own. For he was no man of stormy passions but, rather, a connoisseur. To his taste, neither God nor Nature had done a good enough job: he was needed to put in his two cents. In early youth, he had learned to know all the pleasures of life, and now, as for those principles which for other mortals are commandments, he despised them from the bottom of his soul. So it was also not enough for him that this pretty girl, robbed of her human dignity, should simply sin – uninhibited and with a light heart – when she gave herself over to his desires. He wanted her to recognize what she was doing, so he could behold the gentle suffering of a lost soul and gloat over it. He therefore didn't let himself smile either in word or look but presented himself as a Confessor and asked her straight out if hunger had brought her here.

"No, no. I've had enough to eat ever since I can remember. In our home there was meat three times a week."

That was of course what he'd thought. No one who saw her could have imagined that she'd ever had to go hungry.

"But you were tormented by dreams – heavy, bad? – You came here to enjoy your youth?"

"God, no. Stop asking! Do you live here in Zurich or are you just here in passing?"

"Just here in passing. – Are your parents still living?"

"Yes, but they don't know where I am."

"Not even that you're in Zurich?"

"No, they know nothing about me."

"So what's your name?"

"I am called Martha."

"Martha? I see. Yes there are many Marthas in God's world. So I knew you must be Martha."

"If you write me a letter, you can address it just to Martha, and be sure I'll get it, all my friends do that."

"And your last name?"

"I wouldn't tell you if you put a knife to my throat. I'd rather be killed than speak my father's name here."

"So how did you get here?"

"I'll tell you some other time, but not today, please."

"Too much work to do at home? Had to get up early and scrub the steps?"

"I always enjoyed working."

"Really, is it such a delight? – You have it a lot more comfortable here."

"Oh, why do you say that? – I'll tell you what brought me here. You must be taking pity on me. Most men that come here only want to hear obscenities. They tell you to shut up as soon as you say anything that's not wheedling and flattery. God knows I've never spoken of it to a single soul, and yet I think of nothing else night and day. What consoles me is this: here, it must all soon end. And then it's over and forgotten."

"Don't you believe in a hereafter?"

"For rich people there may be, and good people, not for the likes of us. But that would be so frightful!"

And the young girl again looked deep into his eyes for she was still not quite sure whether he was making fun of her openheartedness. Then she put out the light and proceeded: "I was fourteen years old when my mother brought me to the shop. I had no waist as yet – no figure at all – and my eyes were still big like a calf's eyes. There were four of us, four apprentices, Resi, Cilly, Kathi and I.

As early as Monday morning we were all counting the days till Sunday. On Sunday afternoon we visited each other, drank coffee at home, and then went for a walk in the English Garden. Do you know the English Garden in Munich?"

"Yes, yes. I've often gone skating on the pond with my little girl."

"You didn't have to bring *that* up – now."

"So what did you talk about when the four of you took a walk?"

"Mostly about the manageress. She was so smart, we all took her for some kind of supreme being. When a lady would show up – for the first time – she would take one look at her and immediately cut out all pieces of the bodice on her knees. It was like she sketched her with the scissors."

"You talked of nothing else?"

"Why? Oh, yes we did. Each of us talked of her family at

home. Cilly had a brother that she made clothes for. He was still in school. She helped him with his homework sometimes. You'd never believe how proud of him she was. Now, when I'm alone, I often think: if only I had a child, which always makes me think of little Hans, he was so pretty."

"Well, don't cry!"

"That's not why I'm crying. I'm just thinking how afraid of it I was. And now I'd be so happy. I'd have got something out of it, at least."

"But you'd only spoil the child."

"Yes, you're right, I'd pamper it, I'd love it so frightfully. *My* child must have a better time of it than any other!"

"Do you still love *him*?"

"Oh, yes. I trust you. I could tell you everything."

"How did you get to know him?"

"It was the middle of winter, nine o'clock at night. I'd been in the shop two years. I was wearing long skirts now and when I crossed the street, hatless with my apron on, the men turned their heads. I laughed because I took it as flattery, but didn't give it much of a thought. Then one evening the Directress gave me a gown for the Baroness Libra on Schwabing Road. I was going to go by tram but the trams were all full. It was so stormy, bricks were falling off the chimneys, and it was freezing cold. Everyone wore hooded coats but I only had my jacket with the big buttons and a feather hat that I had to hold on to or it would blow away. Already in Theatiner Street I was wishing I'd never been born. I couldn't feel my hands or feet, and I collided with someone at every step. Once it turned out to be a lamp post. My umbrella got smashed up against it. The wind blew the umbrella away in fragments, and the snow got into my skirts and ran down my neck. I was drenched from head to toe like a little wet dog.

"In front of the Cenotaph [Feldherrnhalle], the strap around my parcel snapped, and the gown fell out into the snow. I wished I was dead! I picked up the gown, wiped the snow off the paper with my handkerchief so it wouldn't sink in. I was then about to put the parcel under my arm. A gust of wind came and drove my skirts up above the knees. O my God, I thought, I do hope no one saw!

"At that moment a gentleman came to me and asked if he might carry my parcel and I said. Yes.

"In this manner we went out together to Schwabing Road and he then accompanied me back to our house on Sendling Street. All he had told me was that he worked in a store and supported his sixty year old mother with his wages. I'd also told him where I work. I had hardly taken a look at him, and would never in my life have recognized him later.

"But next evening when I left the shop he was beside me again as soon as I'd said goodbye to the others. He was so friendly, I couldn't send him away. And so it came about. Every evening he brought me back to the door, and told me how kind and good he was to his mother. And when spring came, he told me one evening that he loved me. At first I didn't believe it. But for a whole month he spoke of nothing else, and then all of a sudden he asked me if I also loved him and I said, Yes.

"That was what was so awful: from that day on, he was not the same. Before this he was always so gentle and good. No more. He now claimed it wasn't true that I loved him. I said: "yes it is, I swear to God! "And it was just as I said. All day at the shop I thought of nothing but him – what kind of a face he'd show me when: we saw each other again It was not the same face any more. He rolled his eyes downwards like he'd swallowed a fly. Often he didn't speak one word all the way home. Previously he'd often kissed me goodbye. Now he didn't even do this. I asked him to, but he wouldn't. He called me a coquette. I was shocked. I didn't know what that was. At first I couldn't remember the word. Then I wrote it down and asked Cilly, and Cilly told me that's what the girls are who walk the streets at night. Cocottes.

"Mother asked me why I looked so unwell, why I ate nothing, and was so quiet. But I couldn't say anything. I hadn't intended to speak of him at home until we could announce our engagement, but he wasn't earning enough as yet, and we would have to wait till his mother died. But then there was the time he angrily turned his back on me in front of the Town Hall and walked away with his hands in his pockets. I ran after him and flung myself on his neck: "I do love you, too," I said, surely he could see that? He should be like he was before, I'd not done him any harm, he shouldn't torment me in this frightful way. – He muttered: "Prove to me that you love me." I asked him how I could prove that, and he muttered I know very well how and I'm not a child any more, I'm a "coquette" and I'm playing with him, but he's had enough, and won't be made a fool of any longer.

"I couldn't sleep all night. I was asking myself what on earth he could have meant and in what way I had ever shown myself to be ungrateful to him. Finally I decided to ask Cilly – since he didn't wish to tell me himself. But, as for telling Cilly the whole story, no, I couldn't do that. No one in the world had noticed my dealings with him, and that's the way I wanted it till we could publicly announce our engagement. He would tell me sometimes that his mother's condition was critical. Then she was better again.

"After lunch I was walking arm in arm with Cilly, and I asked her if she had ever been in love. She thought for a moment, and then said. Yes. I asked her what she did in such a situation. She said she took a hot footbath. And that helps? She said, yes. And had she done nothing else? No, that had been all – I'd like to have found out more about her love but she laughed and said those were private matters.

"That evening, as he walked me home, I told him: " Now I know, Cilly has told me all," he need only wait till tomorrow. "Good, tomorrow," he said and kissed me at the house door. He was so agreeable like he hadn't been for weeks. I was trembling all evening – Mother might notice I was going to take a footbath. I was so scared! When she went to bed, I slipped into the kitchen in my nightshirt. I'd left the fire on under the boiler. Quietly I filled the basin and stood upright in it. And I felt like I'd never felt before. You wouldn't believe it but I trembled and shook with joy and thought about him all the time, only him, what he would say when he saw me thus transformed. I slipped into bed and slept more sweetly than ever in my life before. But next evening: total misery. First we sank into each other's arms and kissed, and I was nearly crying in sheer happiness. Then he said I should come with him but I said he knew of course that I must go home. He called me a silly stupid animal.

"On Sunday this brought me to go to a fortune teller. I intended to tell her just as little of our love as I'd told Cilly but she had it all out in the open in five minutes. And then she told me: I must of course go with him and refuse him nothing. Then he'll definitely know that I love him. I asked what I owed her, and she asked me how much I had on me. I said 12 Marks and 15 Pfennigs. "Very well," said she," normally, it's true, I get twenty," but she'd be satisfied with what I had, since it was me. She recommended that I come to her again later.

"Next evening I was lying on the bed in my clothes, I'd only taken off my shoes. When eleven struck, I groped my way downstairs. He embraced and kissed me in the hall and took me to his apartment. One hour later he brought me back. God is my witness I couldn't understand why he was so happy. I thought to myself it must be something special about love – it makes a man feel so good to learn he is actually loved by a girl.

"And then I became his lover. In the first week, he said: 'If you really love me, you can't live with your parents any more. If the butcher boys were to catch me in your hallway, they'd kill me.' – I took all my things over at night, and next day in the shop said I had a headache and went out and found myself a room with a bed and two chairs. I didn't go home in the evening. On Sunday my father came. He asked if I was still working at the shop. I said, yes. Then he asked who my lover was. I said: "I won't tell. You can beat me as much as you want but I won't tell." Then he said he'd call the police. I answered, I wasn't afraid of the police, I wasn't afraid of anyone. Then he fell on the bed and wept and shook: I thought his soul would come out of his body. Then he stood up, looked me right in the eye and gave me a frightful slap in the face and left. I haven't seen him since.

"My lover now came to my place every evening. Things were going very badly with his mother, so he had given up the apartment. He needed the money for her medicines and the doctor. Often when this wasn't enough, I also gave him some of mine, but I hadn't much to spare, now that I had to put together dinner for two every night. In the beginning, he'd intended to introduce me to his mother. Now, nothing doing, she was too weak. He feared the joy and excitement would surely kill her on the spot. One time in the shop when the Manageress was away, Resi and Cilly spoke about a girl who had a child. I asked if she'd been married. They said, no. I got a terrible shock. I felt so bad I had to go home. I wept till evening came. Never in my life had I thought that one might have children without being married. When I told him this, he called me a little fool and said he wasn't afraid of anything of the kind. But from that day on, I never had another peaceful moment.

"And then his boss sent him here to Zurich. As we were sitting together in the coach, a girl got in. At first she sat down in the other corner, but when she saw my lover, she gave him such a look, you'd have thought a rocket had shot up before her. She then re-seated herself right opposite him. She said she'd been hired as a waitress here. She was laced up so tight, I was breathless. And she couldn't keep her feet still, and fanned herself with a handkerchief that smelled like a menagerie. Her eyes were popping out of her head. She exchanged looks with my lover which must have meant marvelous things but I didn't get it. Sometimes she threw a glance in my direction and I was dreadfully ashamed. I had on a dress from which all color had faded, my head was covered with a grey shawl, and I drew my shoes under the seat because they'd burst open in the front. She wore brand-new, bright yellow lace boots with gold buttons. Her dress was cut so tight, her knees showed through. She held a reticule on her lap: it contained pralines and a bottle of plum brandy. She offered some of this fare to me too. I didn't want any but my lover said I shouldn't be embarrassed Just before Lindau, when the train suddenly stopped because an axle got hot, she almost sank into his arms. On the steamer I was seasick. How we got to Zurich I can't quite remember.

"Already on the second evening, he went with her to the Concert Hall and didn't come home all night. In the morning, I went out to look for him and when I came back his things were gone. I then looked for him all over town. On every block, I thought he must be just around the corner. Finally I found him on a bench down at the waterfront. I said he should come with me. He said, no, he couldn't, we couldn't live together in Zurich, the police didn't allow it. We'd be arrested if we lived together here without being married. But he'd visit me as often as he could.

"In the next fourteen days, he found the time on exactly three occasions. I had found myself work in the linen business, and sat home all day sewing. When he came for the third time, I asked him where he was living, but he wouldn't tell me. And so I often felt compelled to go out again because I thought I just had to find him since I'd decided I wouldn't go home without him.

"It was nearly eleven one evening when I caught him just

leaving an elegant restaurant. I thrust the question right in his face: "You're living with the waitress." He said, "That's none of your business." I then asked him: "Don't you love me any more?" – It was then that he answered: "How can I still love you if I'm not coming over any more?"– At first I didn't understand. "What do you say?" I asked. He then repeated it: "How can I still love you if we're not together any more?" Everything blurred before my eyes. With my hands in front of my face I ran away. First I must think it over. What did he take love to be if he couldn't love me any more because we no longer lived together? I hadn't loved him any less on that account, I was sure. My feelings and my thoughts – oh, it was like I didn't live in this world any more, he and he alone had become the center of my life. I loved him, I still loved him, I'd have been able to work for him for a lifetime – and he couldn't love me because he wasn't coming over any more? I wasn't a stupid child now. In the time that had passed I'd also come to feel there was something sweet about living together.

"But then the thought came to me all of a sudden that this was the way he'd wanted it from the beginning. I ran down to the lake to drown myself. But that didn't satisfy me. I had such a terrible pain in my breast that the water seemed too friendly, too gentle. I ran through the streets hoping someone would come along and abuse me and drive me out of my mind. I felt that, if someone would only take to kicking me, my pain would get less. I had to be degraded so deep down – as deep as possible – till I could no longer feel the claws that were strangling my heart.

"For a long time I was thinking. A gentleman came and stroked my hair. Maybe I would have gone with him. But he was too friendly, too decent. He wore kid gloves, and seemed like someone trying to save me. No, no, I must go down, down, where one sees and hears nothing any more. I told myself I must become so miserable I can't feel my trouble any more.

"My lover had told me there are women in Zurich who

take in young girls in order to sell them and suck their blood dry. I asked a policeman who saw me sitting at the streetcorner where such a woman would be found. He asked me if I'd been there before, and I said, yes. Whereupon he took my arm and led me off to the police station. There sat a gentleman with a red face, a black moustache and blue glasses who also asked me if I'd been with such a woman before. Again I said, yes. Then he asked where, and I pointed somewhere or other with my finger: "I'm a stranger here, this is the first day I've been out, and I can't find my way back." At that he had two policemen take me on and bring me here. So that is how I got here."

"But you can live pretty well here, no?"

"At first the Madam was dissatisfied with me because I always looked so gloomy. But since she noticed that the most repulsive customers always choose me and I never tell them No, since that time she likes me just as well as the cheerful, clever Mademoiselle Palmyra who's here with me."

It was Sunday on the following morning when the young man again found himself in the open. The bells were ringing. Men, women, and children came out of church. The young man would have liked to make a joke to himself but the words stuck in his throat. He'd never felt so small and so good, both at the same time. He compared the sunny, carefree mood of the churchgoers who had just heard their preacher and were looking forward to a good Sunday dinner with the seriousness in his own soul and, without a spark of frivolity or coquetry; he confessed to himself that he did not envy them. When he'd gone over there the previous evening, he had planned to play the part of a Confessor, but now it seemed to him that he had been eavesdropping on a Confessor and he had learned to believe in innocence where he had least looked for it. When he thought back to the girl, he had to despise himself. Without having wished to do anything bad, she had drawn the unlucky card. Never in his life had he wished to do anything good yet he was not totally lost: that was his feeling now. An impression that remained with him for life.

**EROS TWO**

1.
On Mount Olympus one fine day
Eros (Amour, amor, amor*e*)
Looked around
And found
Stretched out in an arbor there
Venus Urania, Fairest of the Fair.

2.
Nine days later (odd but true)
Venus gave birth to Eros Two
And he was born (this too is odd)
A fullgrown god
His father's passion in his face,
In his body all his mother's grace.

3.
But amour etcetera was not his thing
He liked to dance and sing.
Rather than amour, amore
He'd write a sonnet or a story
Then, afterwards, dine
With the Muses Nine.

4.
Eros One some time ago
Gave his young son a certain bow
Shooting his arrow (Cupid's dart)
Eros Two impales your heart
With the love of art.

# Also by
# Eric Bentley...

## Mother Courage and Her Children

**By Bertolt Brecht**
**English version by Eric Bentley**

*Morality / 18m, 5f, extras / Int., 5 Exts.*
Brecht follows Mother Courage and her children through twelve years of the holy war of the early seventeenth century through Sweden, Poland, Finland, Bavaria, and Italy. Mother Courage's first son is a dolt, but he makes a dashing soldier and plunderer. Her second son is honest, and he meets an early death from a firing squad. His name is Swiss Cheese. So now Mother Courage and her dumb daughter follow the armies with their wagon and wares, as first one side then another wins. They acquire in their train a chaplain and a cook. Until, one day, peace is declared. But it is too brief. The plundering soldier son is brought to shame, and the daughter who would be married is shot instead. War is resumed; for it seems that, like love, it is perpetual.

Please visit our website **samuelfrench.com** for complete descriptions and licensing information.

www.ingramcontent.com/pod-product-compliance
Lightning Source LLC
Chambersburg PA
CBHW070649300426
44111CB00013B/2341